MOZART

SYMPHONY IN G MINOR, K. 550

The Score of the New Mozart Edition

Historical Note

Analysis · Views and Comments

NORTON CRITICAL SCORES

BACH   **CANTATA NO. 4**
edited by Gerhard Herz

BACH   **CANTATA NO. 140**
edited by Gerhard Herz

BEETHOVEN   **SYMPHONY NO. 5 IN C MINOR**
edited by Elliot Forbes

BERLIOZ   **FANTASTIC SYMPHONY**
edited by Edward T. Cone

CHOPIN   **PRELUDES, OPUS 28**
edited by Thomas Higgins

DEBUSSY   **PRELUDE TO "THE AFTERNOON OF A FAUN"**
edited by William W. Austin

MOZART   **PIANO CONCERTO IN C MAJOR, K. 503**
edited by Joseph Kerman

MOZART   **SYMPHONY IN G MINOR, K. 550**
edited by Nathan Broder

PALESTRINA   **POPE MARCELLUS MASS**
edited by Lewis Lockwood

PURCELL   **DIDO AND AENEAS**
edited by Curtis Price

SCHUBERT   **SYMPHONY IN B MINOR ("UNFINISHED")**
edited by Martin Chusid

SCHUMANN   **DICHTERLIEBE**
edited by Arthur Komar

STRAVINSKY   **PETRUSHKA**
edited by Charles Hamm

WAGNER   **PRELUDE AND TRANSFIGURATION**
from *TRISTAN AND ISOLDE*
edited by Robert Bailey

Wolfgang Amadeus Mozart

SYMPHONY IN G MINOR
K. 550

The Score of the New Mozart Edition
Historical Note
Analysis · Views and Comments

Edited by
NATHAN BRODER

W · W · NORTON & COMPANY
New York · London

Library of Congress Catalog Card No. 67-17011

Published simultaneously in Canada by
George J. McLeod Limited, Toronto

W. W. Norton & Company, Inc., 500 Fifth Avenue, New York, N.Y. 10110

ISBN 0-393-09775-7

PRINTED IN THE UNITED STATES OF AMERICA

4 5 6 7 8 9 0

Contents

Historical Note

In the first half of 1788, when Mozart was at the height of his creative powers, his everyday circumstances suddenly began to deteriorate. Although he had recently been appointed a composer to the Imperial court, the salary was only 800 gulden (something under $400) a year and the duties light. Two or three years previously Mozart had given frequent concerts and had plenty of pupils; he had triumphed in Prague with *Figaro* in 1786 and *Don Giovanni* in 1787. Now his fortunes went into a slump. When *Don Giovanni* was performed for the first time in Vienna, on May 7, 1788, it aroused mixed reactions; although it was given fifteen times that year, it does not seem to have been regarded as a success in Vienna. In 1785 Leopold Mozart had been told by a Salzburg journalist: "It is really astonishing to see what a number of compositions your son is publishing. In all the announcements of musical works I see nothing but Mozart"; now in the spring of 1788 Wolfgang could not obtain enough subscribers to a set of three string quintets, and the projected publication was first postponed and then abandoned. In June Mozart planned a series of public concerts, but these apparently did not take place. Indeed, as Deutsch points out, Mozart was never again to give a public concert in Vienna. In June, too, begin the letters to Mozart's friend and brother Mason, Michael Puchberg, and others, asking for loans.

Nevertheless he continued to compose, with his characteristic incredible speed. The thematic index he had begun to keep in 1784 contains entries for the following works during the first half of 1788, in addition to smaller pieces and dances: on January 3, the Allegro and Andante for piano, K. 533; on February 24, the Piano Concerto in D, K. 537; on March 4 the soprano aria *Ah se in ciel*, K. 538; on April 24,

28, and 30 the three new pieces for the Vienna production of *Don Giovanni: Dalla sua pace,* for tenor, the duet *Per queste tue manine,* and *Mi tradì quell' alma ingrata,* for soprano; on June 22 the Trio in E, K. 542; on June 26 the Symphony in E-flat, K. 543; on July 14 the Trio in C, K. 548; on July 25 the Symphony in G minor, K. 550; and on August 10 the Symphony in C, K. 551.

Deutsch suggests that the three symphonies may have been written for the planned series of concerts, which never materialized. There is no record of a performance of any of these symphonies during the three years of life left to Mozart. It seems very likely, however, that at least the G minor was played while he was still alive. Mozart originally scored the work for flute, pairs of oboes, bassoons, and horns, and strings. At some later time he added two clarinets and rewrote the oboe parts to accommodate them. It is highly improbable that he would have gone to that trouble unless there was a definite performance in view. H. C. Robbins Landon, the editor of the score printed here, speculates that the change may have been made for a pair of concerts that took place on April 16 and 17, 1791, conducted by Antonio Salieri; a "grand symphony" by Mozart was played, and it is known that his friends, the clarinetists Anton Stadler and his younger brother Johann, performed in the orchestra. Both versions, the one with clarinets and the one without, are still in use. The first edition was published in 1794, three years after Mozart's death, by Johann André in Offenbach. André bought many Mozart manuscripts from the composer's widow. André's grandson sold the autograph of the symphony to Princess Anna of Hesse; the Princess presented it to Brahms, in appreciation of his dedicating to her his Piano Quintet, Op. 34; and Brahms left it to the Society of the Friends of Music in Vienna, in whose library it still reposes today.

The Symphony is popularly known as "No. 40," because that is the number given it in the old Breitkopf & Härtel Complete Edition of Mozart's works. Actually, according to the most recent authoritative listing, it is the 47th of Mozart's complete symphonies. In the scholarly literature it is always referred to by its key, plus—if there is any possibility of confusion with the "little" G minor Symphony of 1773, K. 183— its year of composition or Köchel number.

THE SCORE

OF THE SYMPHONY

Edited by

H. C. ROBBINS LANDON

Textual Note [†]

The present edition of the Symphony in G minor, K. 550, prepared from the Urtext of the *Neue Mozart-Ausgabe,* in its second version with clarinets, is based on the autograph of the first version of 1788 and the autograph wind-score. Certain secondary manuscript sources and the André first edition of the parts (without clarinets) (1794) were compared with these two main sources.

The first print appears to have been made, if not from the autograph itself (which is very likely), then from an extremely careful copy of it. The evidence for this, as well as a detailed enumeration of all the sources used, is to be found in the Critical Report to the *Neue Mozart-Ausgabe,* Series IV, Group 11, Vol. 9. Mozart's autograph is most precise and shows clearly the composer's intentions. A few problems, however, call for general comment:

1. Parallel passages: Like Haydn and Beethoven, Mozart generally wrote out his recapitulations from memory. Despite his extraordinary memory one often finds small differences in phrasing between the exposition and the recapitulation. In general, Mozart's autograph was followed even in apparent inconsistencies and it remains for the conductor himself to make such changes as he considers necessary.

2. Mozart's notation of two, three, and four-part chords in the strings: In the second half of the 18th century it appeared to be general practice to write chords for strings with two or more stems. It cannot be decided with absolute certainty whether Mozart intended "divisi" performance or if this was merely a method of notation. It is probable, however, that the latter obtains. Three-part chords were usually noted by Mozart as follows:

𝅘𝅥, 𝅘𝅥, 𝅘𝅥, or 𝅘𝅥.

Most of these cases were judged to be chords and not "divisi"; occasionally such chords were noted by Mozart with one stem.

† From H. C. Robbins Landon's Preface to the Bärenreiter pocket score based on the *Neue Mozart-Ausgabe* (Kassel, 1958, pp. xi–xii).

3. The oft-occurring combination of ties and slurs was left unchanged in Mozart's original notation, thus

♩♪|♪♩♩ and not ♩ ♪|♪ ♩ ♩,

since this was considered a clear presentation of his accurate and careful phrasing.

4. Mozart's division of cross-beams and stems was retained wherever possible. Contradictory parallel passages were generally reconciled and the deviation noted in the Critical Report.

5. Mozart's different methods of writing dots and elongated or thickened strokes present every editor of a Mozart work with a difficult task. The decision whether to print an accent or a dot in this new edition could not easily be made in many cases. (Mozart's intentional accents [strokes], which in performance are to be regarded as short accents, have been printed as wedgeshaped accents, according to modern practice.)

6. It is a principle of the *Neue Mozart-Ausgabe,* from which the present separate edition is reproduced, to indicate editorial additions in the score; in this connection the use of "a 2" in unison passages for pairs of wind instruments (engraved on one staff for the present edition) needs special explanation. The indication "a 2" is not to be regarded in the strict sense as an editorial addition, but simply as a rewriting of the instruments noted in the original on two staves. On these grounds the indication "a 2" is printed in normal and not in italic type.

Editorial additions and completions are given as sparingly as possible and are distinguishable as follows:

Letters (particularly dynamic and agogic signs) in italics.
Accidentals in square brackets.
Accents and dots in small print.
Phrasing in dotted lines.

ACKNOWLEDGMENT

This edition of Mozart's G minor Symphony, K. 550 (2nd version), is printed by permission of Bärenreiter-Verlag Kassel-Basel-Paris-London from *W. A. Mozart, Neue Ausgabe sämtlicher Werke, herausgegeben in Verbindung mit den Mozart-Städten Augsburg, Salzburg und Wien von der Internationalen Stiftung Mozarteum Salzburg, Serie IV, Werkgruppe 11, Sinfonien-Band 9* (BA 4509), edited by H. C. Robbins Landon. The text of the Neue Mozart-Ausgabe has also been published by Bärenreiter in a separate score (BA 4724), a pocket score (TP 40), and the complete performing materials (BA 4724).

INSTRUMENTATION

1 Flute (*Flauto*)
2 Oboes
2 Clarinets in B♭ (*Si♭*)
2 Bassoons (*Fagotti*)
2 Horns (*Corni*) : in B♭ alto (*Si♭ alto*) in I and IV, G (*Sol*) in I. III, and IV, and E♭ (*Mi♭*) in II

Violin I
Violin II
Viola
Violoncello
Double Bass

SYMPHONY IN G MINOR, K. 550

I: Molto Allegro

I: Molto Allegro

unison

chromatic rising
pattern

Cadence - affected by chromaticism
→ B♭M

Diatonic scale

Fmi

(also thematic)
closing material

Coda

MENUETTO
Allegretto

hemiola

3-bar phrase length.
3 + 3 + 3 + phrase extension

Flauto

Oboi

Clarinetti
in Si♭

Fagotti

Corni
in Sol

Violino I

Violino II

Viola

Violoncello
e Basso

Gmi

7

Dmi

III: Menuetto

like a development section – tonal ambiguity

phrase extension

contrapuntal imitation

end of A section.

Gmi

cadential material — reinforce the tonic.

look back to Dmi briefly

TRIO - features the wind more.

GM

Question / answer ⎫ antiphony
call / response ⎭

PM

phrase extension

D.C. Menuetto

ANALYSIS

Unless specified otherwise, all numbered footnotes in the following essays are those of the author. References in the essays to measure numbers have been changed to conform to the numbering used in this edition.

HERMANN ABERT

[*The G minor Symphony*] †

For the principal formal analysis of the symphony I have chosen the one by Hermann Abert. There are, of course, many ways in which to analyze such a work, and the theorists do not often agree. Two parts of the symphony, the development sections of the first and last movements, have baffled them all. There are many *descriptions* of what happens in these sections, but no analyst known to me, not even Heinrich Schenker, has given a satisfactory explanation of the *function* of each occurrence there in terms of the whole organism. Nevertheless, of all the published analyses, it seems to me that Abert's is the richest, the most generally intelligible, and perhaps the most provocative. (Saint-Foix, to whom all Mozart research is indebted, has nothing essential to add to Abert concerning our symphony.)

The analysis is taken from Abert's monumental revision of the great pioneering biography of Mozart by Otto Jahn. The first edition of Jahn was published in four volumes from 1856 to 1859. It went through four editions and then, for the fifth edition (2 vols., 1919–21), Abert rewrote it completely, retaining some of Jahn's material but adding a great deal that was new.

There are no sharper·contrasts in Mozart's instrumental works than between those two symphonies [the E-flat major, K. 543, and the G minor, K. 550]. The dark, pessimistic mood struck in the first movement of the G minor Piano Quartet and then resumed in intensified degree in the String Quintet suffuses this symphony to its bitter end. Contemporary hearers immediately grasped this character, if occasionally with quite mixed feelings; but it is very indicative of the attitude towards Mozart

† From *W. A. Mozart*, Leipzig, 1956, II, 479–90, by permission of VEB Breitkopf & Härtel Musikverlag, Leipzig. Translation by the editor. Some of Abert's footnotes have been omitted, as have music examples that can be easily found in the score.

in the Romantic era that the work was then usually considered charming and gay, indeed even unimportant.[1] It is only in more recent times that this view, which naturally had a decisive effect on performance also, was corrected to conform to that of Mozart and his time.[2]

The symphony begins without an introduction, with only a one-measure anticipation of the accompaniment. The theme at first follows a melodic type that is a favorite of the period and that later is especially prominent in *Die Zauberflöte:* [3]

But, for one thing, it extends the upbeats (NB) by tripling them, without depriving them of their character as upbeats—for the main accent remains on the third and seventh measures of the theme—and, for another, in connection with this, the high note of the leap of a sixth comes on the weak beat of the measure. While the melody-type is thus already deprived of much of its original energy, this change in its character is intensified by the fact that the extended upbeat is differentiated rhythmically and melodically:

1. Thus H. Hirschbach, in the *Neue Zeitschrift für Musik,* VIII, 190, characterizes "this so-called symphony" as an "ordinary, mild piece of music, as unprepossessing in invention as in workmanship, which (if one sets aside all the deeper requirements of our time) could not have been very difficult to write and which Beethoven seems not to have regarded as so great a masterpiece." Robert Schumann, too, laid bare the difference between then and now especially clearly when he criticized D. F. Schubart's esthetics of tonalities: "In G minor he [Schubart] finds dissatisfaction, uneasiness, torment over an unfortunate plan, ill-humored gnawing at the bit. Now compare Mozart's G minor Symphony, *that Greek lightness and grace [diese griechisch schwebende Grazie]* . . . and see!" (*Gesammelte Schriften,* 5th ed. [Kreisig], I, 105.) The Swabian theologian Chr. Palmer still finds (*Evangelische Hymnologie,* 1865, p. 246) nothing in the symphony but "joy and animation." It is the same Romanticism that stamped Beethoven as a "Titan," although his art is far more than Titanism.

2. The Romantic view lingered on well into our century. As late as 1927, an analyst could write of the first movement: "It is compact of 'the soothing thoughts that spring out of human suffering' "; of the Minuet that it "is more simply regarded as a jolly excursus on the opening theme"; and of the finale: "The verve of this movement is tremendous. It . . . is the best possible tonic for the low in spirits. 'No more shall grief of mine the season wrong.' " (A. F. Dickinson, *A Study of Mozart's Last 3 Symphonies,* London, 1927.)—At the same time it must be pointed out that even in the 19th century there were some writers attuned to the idiom of Mozart's time. Otto Jahn was one (Abert's account is based on Jahn's, which was originally published in 1859); see also the extract from Oulibicheff given here (p. 105). [*Editor*]

3. The aria *Dies Bildnis ist bezaubernd schön.* [*Editor*]

melodically through the heavy sigh motif NB, rhythmically through that motif's anapestic character, whose forward-driving force, in this environment, has nothing in it of affirmation of life but from the beginning strikes a mood of unrest and tension.[4] The pervasive feminine cadences are characteristic too. The theme shows the same broad curve as the corresponding one of the E-flat Symphony. But the second part of its antecedent [mm. 9–20] shows a very considerable increase in emotional effect, caused by the metrical extension and the sharp delineation of the half-cadence on the dominant: here the passion that was up to this point restrained with effort, breaks out with open ferocity.

The consequent of the theme is interrupted after its first group [m. 28] by the extremely combative transition group of the tutti. We are already in B-flat major, the key of the subordinate theme. But this must first be secured by conflict. So B-flat is transformed into the subdominant of F major, and the harmonic development of this group proceeds within F major in the usual succession IV-V-I, except that the concluding F major itself immediately achieves the force of a dominant. Hovering over the whole section, therefore, is the harmonic progression:

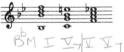

which then appears bodily, as it were, in the subordinate theme. From this group, then, which is anything but a merely mechanical connecting

4. This interpretation of the whole first measure of the theme as an extended upbeat is not very helpful. The "upbeat" alone, without the leap, is the basis of an important section of the development, as will be seen. In this connection a sheet of sketches by Mozart, now in Tokyo, for works completed in 1787 and 1788, is of interest. It contains the following theme scored for string quintet with two violas, clearly a foreshadowing of the symphony theme:

See Sidney Newman, *Mozart's G minor Quintet (K. 516) and Its Relationship to the G minor Symphony (K. 550)*, in *Music Review*, XVII (1956), 287. [*Editor*]

link, *this* particular subordinate theme, immanent in the character of the whole passage, flings itself free. The eloquent whole-measure rest, too, is not accidental: anyone who is at all susceptible to a musical experience will find, during this sudden silence, a mood setting in that makes the entry of the subordinate theme feel necessary to him.

In its investiture, this theme [m. 44 ff.] is a particularly lovely example of the Classic relationship between strings and winds. Indeed, the alternating predominance of different combinations already leads here to modern "filigree" work—that is, to the dividing of a theme among various instrumental groups. In its character, however, this theme reduces the agitation of the principal theme to a moving plaint. This meditation, however, is brief. The development section does not touch upon it at all, and when the idea floats back in the recapitulation, it takes on, within the dark G minor mood, the stamp of deepest resignation, a gripping illustration of the profoundly human content that this movement bears within it. An inspired creative force is also evident in the closing extension of the theme with its bemused dip down towards A-flat major,[5] which, to be sure, with the return of B-flat major at once produces the natural reaction.[6] The closing section of the theme-group [m. 72 ff.] returns to the material of the principal theme; the winds cling to its sigh motif in imitative play while the strings, also in imitation, emit a heavy, groaning sob.[7] This more intimate section too, and with it the whole theme-group, is concluded with peevish defiance. In the repetition of all these themes there is always an interchange of orchestral groups or, as in the last, double counterpoint, which now plays an important part in the development section too.

This section differs from all the others in that it never shakes off the principal theme but savors every aspect of that musical experience, instead of, as in the E-flat Symphony, giving itself up to the alternation of individual moods. In Mozart's fashion it begins with a transition as surprising as it is laconic, which leads us, in a manner that seems sudden but is inwardly entirely justified by what has gone before, to the remote,

---

5. This alleged progression in the direction of A-flat major would be hard to justify. The A♭ in m. 68 is simply the seventh of the B-flat major chord horizontalized in mm. 66–68. [*Editor*]

6. Only the unison [mm. 66–68] is related to the chromaticism of the subordinate theme.

7. This semitone figure, ultimately derived from the semitone in the "upbeat" of the principal theme, is an outgrowth of a figure that had appeared in slightly different shapes earlier: m. 16 ff., woodwinds; m. 58, flute and bassoons. [*Editor*]

"hot" key of F-sharp minor. Of the main theme we hear from now on only the first eight measures; in a strange anxiety this formation sinks stepwise, the lower melodic line leading from $c\sharp^2$ chromatically through $b\sharp^1\text{-}b^1\text{-}a\sharp^1\text{-}a^1$ to g^1, supported by the corresponding steps in the bassoons and basses. Now [m. 114] there is an explosion with the entrance of the theme, forte, in the basses in E minor—but without any transition. Simultaneously, a counterpoint in staccato eighth notes, in whose first measures echoes the chordal motif of the transition group. A powerful effect is exerted in the first half by the suspension harmonies of the winds, in the second half by the violent forcing-apart of theme and counterpoint. And now the unfettered passion calms down in double counterpoint over the regular harmonic progression E minor, A minor, D minor, G minor, C major, F major, and B-flat major and does not halt until it reaches the dominant of D minor [m. 134], where the first part of the theme, which has been tossed about through all the keys and is now condensed to the·semitone step of its sigh motif, closes the whole section like a shrill cry. This constitutes the climax of emotional tension in the development. From the technical standpoint a clear indication of Mozart's contrapuntal tendencies, at that time awakening with growing strength in him, it differs for precisely that reason from Haydn, for whom counterpoint was simply a station on the road towards his new thematic development. But here, after the soft melodic gliding of the preceding, the sudden outburst of counterpoint works with dramatic force. As it had entered, without any dynamic transition, so the section vanishes and now gives way to thematic working-out in Haydn's sense, so that we find in this section all types of development brought together: melodic spinning-out, counterpoint, and modern thematic working-out.

The only thing that remains is the final member of the theme, which now [m. 138] continues its sighs alone and piano in the first violins, as though helpless. But now the winds intensify this moving plaint to the point of self-torment; the original sigh motif, which hitherto has appeared only in purely melodic form, is harmonized from now on, and indeed with a sharpness that constantly increases up to the end of the development. With the hand of a true master the instrumentation is here made to serve the expression: hopelessly the first violin struggles upward over the dark sound of the sustained bassoon and oboe tones [8]

---

8. Bassoon and clarinet in the revised version. [*Editor*]

and each time at the end of its phrase undergoes, through the entrance of the two higher winds, the intensification of expression mentioned above. Even though the violin, after the melodic line is turned downwards again, finds its natural support in the other strings [9] once more, the winds, with their cuttingly dissonant echoes, remain the true bearers of painful agitation. The harmony too is constantly in a state of unrest in this section. Not until the tutti section enters, once again suddenly [m. 152], is solid ground regained, with the dominant of G minor. Nothing remains now of the principal theme but its basic motif, which the strings take over from the last call in the winds, while the winds return to the old transition ideas. There follows here a new climax of tension, which concentrates the expression on the simplest possible basic and germ ideas of the whole movement—one can now see what logic governs this development. As far as the modulation scheme is concerned, nothing would now stand in the way of the recapitulation. But Mozart follows the last outbreak of agitation too with a quiet echo, which serves at the same time as a bridge to the return of the beginning. Only the sforzati of the bassoons [m. 160 ff.] refer to what has preceded; over them, however, the basic motif sinks in a chromatic line in the winds, its last note extended to triple its original value: it is the weariest, the most resigned passage in the whole movement; [10] this gives the return of the main theme [m. 164], which is pushed through a sharp dissonance and strongly emphasizes its own dominant character, the effect of a redemption. Thus this development intensifies the spiritual properties of the theme group in every direction: a powerful climax of agitation in the center, flanked by two sections of the same general character but more restrained in expression, all three differentiated from one another in the manner in which they are dealt with [11] and yet offshoots of the same trunk and bearers of a single, organically evolving emotional state— there is scarcely a Mozartean development that is borne along with the

9. Cellos instead of basses point here to an echo of the old concertino groups.

10. This progression in the woodwinds was foreshadowed by a similar, shorter one at the beginning of the development, and before that by a still shorter one in the bassoons in mm. 20–21. A final echo of the procedure introduces the coda (m. 285). All of these passages, but especially that of the bassoons in mm. 20–21, represent an important contribution that Mozart made to orchestral music: the use of the special color of individual wind instruments to enhance the emotional effect of a passage. This kind of writing for orchestra had been known earlier in the opera and in sacred choral music but Mozart seems to have been the first to apply it successfully to purely orchestral music. [*Editor*]

11. The difference extends as far as key and instrumentation.

same spiritual energy.[12]

This now reaches over into the recapitulation, whose expressiveness is heightened by variants and extensions to a far greater degree than its predecessor in E-flat major. The main theme itself receives an addition by the winds, but above all it is the old "transition group" that is very significantly extended. The goal of the process is the subordinate theme, whose present key of G minor was in Mozart's mind's eye from the beginning as surely as it was in the corresponding String Quintet. But this important change must be inwardly prepared and motivated. In this lies the significance of the varied transition-group, which, the theme-group having turned to E-flat major, begins in that key [m. 191] but then shifts towards F minor and finally through wild strettos of the quarter-note motif [13] reaches G minor [m. 211] in order to repeat in that key the entire section in its earlier version.[14] The subordinate theme itself, which only now achieves its full expression, has already been discussed; its closing too is extended, in a way, by an intensified energy of expression. The closing group [m. 260 ff.] proceeds in regular fashion at first, but in *its* conclusion, likewise extended, once more condenses the two fundamental contrasts of the movement, wild outbreaks [15] and resigned ebbing of feeling. To this is linked the true coda [m. 285], which here has the effect not only of affirming the conclusion but of rounding off the whole feeling-content of the movement with psychological consistency. The main theme returns, but its second part dissolves, as it were, in inert syncopation; the entries in imitation are intended only to intensify the feeling of resignation. Only then does the final little section break out, once more violently confirming the old opposing spirits. The anapestic rhythm extends its force into the final chord:

12. For other analyses of this section, see Arnold Schoenberg, *Structural Functions of Harmony*, New York, 1954, p. 149 ff., and Heinrich Schenker, *Das Meisterwerk in der Musik*, II (1926), 109 ff. The Schenker study, which analyzes the entire symphony, takes for granted a thorough understanding of his *Urlinie* system. [*Editor*]

13. In the new counterpointing motif:

may be seen a reference to the melodic line of the principal theme (see above).

14. Further concerning this passage, see Arnold Schoenberg's outline, reproduced below on p. 101. [*Editor*]

15. This section too is thematic.

The Andante is closely related to this movement in form and expression. It is in a sonata form of the same thematic unity, and corres-
ponds to the first movement also in the important part played by counterpoint. That it belongs to the same area of emotional experience is shown
at the start by its principal theme [16] with its weighty tone-repetitions,
which are only intensified by the imitation, the heavy suspensions, and
under them the oppressively twisting chromatic bass-progression. Indeed
the consequent's reply almost causes the emotion to overflow in the
Paisiello-like motif [m. 5], but in its second phrase this motif is quite
suddenly broken up; even the horns, which have accompanied the soaring of feeling, become silent, and in painful chromaticism the forephrase
of the whole theme comes to an end. The thirty-second-note motif, however, which is so strikingly introduced [m. 7], achieves a decisive significance, almost like the sigh motif in the first movement, as the real bearer
of agitation against the musing, contemplative lines of the theme. In
the consequent of the whole theme [m. 9 ff.] there is an immediate intensification, especially through the use of double counterpoint; it has
at the very beginning a heavy pedalpoint, over which the motif previously in the bass becomes a moving song of sorrow in the first violins;
this is followed by one of those "singing basses" (with the theme) that
are characteristic for the last three symphonies. Only the ending rises
again to greater assurance, thanks to the motif introduced from above.
In the second theme, which begins without transition on the dominant
[m. 20], the pressure latent in the first one builds to an open explosion
—or at least tries to, for here again, and as early as the second measure,
there is a fluttered scattering by that thirty-second-note motif. But this
motif does not merely interrupt; it also constructs. It now takes the lead,
first calming the waves but then, after the F major close [m. 27], un-
expectedly leading over to the D-flat major section; there it entwines
fragrant tendrils around the first motif of the main theme, which now
enters as if in a dream. A hint of nature begins to appear here, but soon
[m. 33] a mighty rushing rises in the full orchestra, out of which, at the
lovely turn towards B-flat major, that ivy-like motif climbs proudly. But

16. Notice that all the main themes of this symphony begin with an upbeat.
The melodic outline of the first period of the theme:

is an old favorite of Mozart's, which returns immediately in the finale of the C major
Symphony. The tone-repetition followed by a suspension is related to the third theme
of the Andante of the E-flat Symphony.

again a sudden halt, then there is heard as closing theme [m. 37] an unadulterated sweet call of the nightingale, at first in the strings,[17] then in the winds, as though sounding from different sides and again with that motif frolicking around it; very beautiful and convincing is the expression of sadness that immediately thereafter overflows from the whole orchestra (at the renewed descent to G-flat major [18]). But it is quickly gone. In indescribable sweetness and inwardness, preceded by the entrance of that motif, the section comes to an end.

At the beginning of the development the dark spirits of the main theme announce themselves in a hollow knocking, then in heavy blows again, drawing in their wake that short motif too: anxiously it flutters each time down the chord prescribed for it by the energetic chromatic ascent of the basses. The evenly hammering rhythm of the principal theme is the main bearer of this tension, which expends itself finally on the dominant of C minor [m. 64 f.]. Once more that short motif attempts to disentangle the situation. But the mood was too deeply troubled to achieve this in the sense of a liberation. Soon the main theme returns in the bassoons on a bare, hard fourth—a downright fearful passage—and yet it is immediately replaced by its soft, elegiac counterpoint [m. 70, clarinet] which, with its expressive opening dissonance already pointing towards Romanticism and with the thirty-second-note motif fluttering about it, brings the section to an end. On this track of sorrow the development glides quite secretly into the recapitulation [m. 74]. The whole development thus constitutes a single grand crescendo of feeling, although a crescendo mark never appears in the score; an instructive example of how Mozart deals with problems of this sort in his own way.

The recapitulation soon introduces an inspired extension of the consequent of the theme. That is, it is combined with the second theme; in addition an important part is played by the counterpoint mentioned above, which here takes on almost the style of a recitative. It is only when the theme is taken up by the basses [m. 94]—the low tones in the horns add greatly to the effect here—that the unfolding proceeds in regular fashion, in order to link up closely now to the course of the theme group.[19]

17. Here, too, is a reminiscence of the old contrast between tutti and concertino; it even has the form of the old trio of two violins and viola.

18. It is difficult to see G-flat major anywhere in here. The progression leads clearly to B-flat major. [*Editor*]

19. In the first and last movements of this symphony Mozart calls for one horn in B-flat alto and another in G (obviously for greater flexibility), in the Andante two

The Minuet returns to the mood of conflict of the first movement and intensifies it.[20] This movement, too, does not shake off its basic idea, this one too in its course makes most productive use of the devices of counterpoint. Metrically too it is unusual: its main theme begins with two three-measure phrases, to which the consequent adds a continuation of two measures, to close with a further three-measure phrase. And this relationship continues stubbornly in the second part: here the three-measure members are fastened to each other through imitation, and at the entry of the little epilogue (m. 36 ff. before the end) we feel especially clearly that the rhythmic emphasis of the main theme is not on the first measure but on the second. All this gives the piece the character of a downright crabbed, savage obstinacy. The second section sharpens this rude quality enormously at first, through the hard, strict two-voiced texture, from which there evolves the contrast of richly polyphonic strettos. The various voices do not permit one another to finish, and the theme itself undergoes an important transformation with the turn towards the dominant, which it now maintains. From this comes that epilogue, which presents the theme in its original form. In its manner of expression the epilogue reaches back to the mood of the whole work: even this powerful agitation ends in resignation. Once again the winds are the bearers of the transformation, and again it proceeds with that elegiac, chromatic part-writing which is characteristic of such passages throughout the symphony.

At the same time, however, the epilogue liberates the mood for the sweet sorrow of the Trio. Its theme, which is related to that of the minuet proper,[21] reminds one of a popular song, and its refrain-like little consequent:

---

in E-flat, and in the Minuet two in G. These serve his needs very well, but in the second half of m. 104 in the recapitulation section of the Andante the situation demands stopped notes if the horns are to support the harmony as they did in the exposition. It is the only time in the whole symphony when stopped notes are employed. Mozart was very careful to avoid these imperfect sounds in his symphonies (the only other instances occur in the Andante and Presto of the E-flat Symphony, K. 543), although he did not hesitate to use them in other types of composition. [*Editor*].

20. Hermann Kretzschmar, *Führer durch den Konzertsaal,* I (1887), 186, correctly calls it "one of the most combative movements ever constructed over that old elegant dance form."

21. Compare its beginning with the melodic line of the principal theme:

The beginning of the finale, too, uses the first three notes.

especially, is a familiar visitor from Austrian folk music. The setting is a new and lovely example of Mozart's manner of letting strings and winds concertize with each other, as had long been customary with the Viennese in this section. The winds here always carry the melody considerably farther and cause the feeling of longing to increase markedly; but the final trick is played by the horns, which, reserved until the third section, suddenly envelop the lovely tune in their romantic sounds.

The Allegro assai has for its main theme a regularly constructed two-part song form of 32 measures, which is built dynamically, after the older practice, from the rapid alternation of soli and tutti. Its opening, shooting upward in a triad, belongs to an old type, too, but on the other hand the unprepared suspension into which the motion discharges is individual. It lends the theme at the same time a quality that is somewhat agitated, indeed desperate; the loosed arrow causes a sharp wound right at the start. The wild echo in the tutti with its characteristically Mozartean rhythm of struggle: [22]

is also not absent, this constant alternation of *p* and *f* having about it something strangely agitating, even numbing. One is plainly aware how the basic mood of the whole work is here at last intensified into the wild and daemonic. The tutti, with its motif clearly linked to the close of the first movement, takes over the continuation in the transition group [m. 32 ff.], which is governed by the same rhythmic motif (but without upbeat) and is filled with all sorts of warring eighth-note motifs. But they are no longer, as formerly so frequently, casual, noisy connective elements. For what appears here in addition to that principal motif, which finally wanders into the basses, is thematic:

22. It is clearly reminiscent of the anapestic form of the first movement:

b) comes from the main theme, *a*) on the other hand is identical with an important motif from the analogous section of the first movement.

The subordinate theme is introduced [m. 71] in the old concertino fashion as a trio (two violins and viola). At first it does not bear the stamp of suffering, as did its opposite number in the first movement; instead, with its affective soaring to the subdominant it has the mark of dreamy longing, indeed its first period almost makes one think of a bird-call from nature, as in the Andante. But as early as in the consequent the melodic line is dissolved into that painful chromaticism which we know so well from the other movements of the work; this period is in fact quite strikingly related to its analogue of the first movement. The theme is repeated by the winds with two intensifying upbeats. In the consequent, however, the melodic contours are completely drawn into a heavy chromatic motion involving all the voices, and immediately thereafter [m. 101] the old unrest breaks out again with that tutti motif. Thus the subordinate themes of first and last movements are inwardly unusually closely related; like that of the first Allegro, the one in the finale is ignored in the development section and as a consequence is given in the recapitulation an uncommonly deepened expression.

The beginning of the development section intensifies to the utmost the surprises customary with Mozart at this place, in that after the onslaught of the main theme (with the cutting major seventh) every customary procedure seems to be tossed overboard. The daemonism of the movement manifests itself here with a savagery that induces fear. What is hidden under these unison blows and grotesque intervals is the theme with its constituent members:

But in the heat of passion it is as though this melodic material were stripped to its skeleton, only its outermost contours remain [the pitches marked by asterisks in mm. 3–8], under the pressure of the experience in part metrically displaced (as in mm. 3, 5, 8) or sharpened, as in the slashing triplet (m. 4).[23] Twice there appears a so-called written-out retard (mm. 6–7 and 9–10), the second time in the winds, whose connecting motif in addition clearly points to the analogous wind passage in the first movement. In the contrapuntal construction of what follows, as in the strict concentration upon the main theme, lies a further relationship between the two fast movements. On the other hand, they differ widely in their mood-progression. For the finale does not permit the agitation to calm down after its climax but interrupts it (at the C-sharp minor passage [m. 185]) for a few measures, only in order to whip it up more wildly and to break off the whole thing suddenly before the recapitulation, on the shrill dissonance of the diminished seventh chord.

Almost the entire development proceeds in forte. Only at the beginning is there a softer section, where first violins and winds toss the theme from one to the other; the harmony here drives, on the sharply marked quarter-note rhythm, down the circle of fifths from A minor to F minor. Here [m. 147], on a sharp horn-call, the forte appears and at the same time a new development of the theme, at first two-part, with an extension by means of the scale-motif:

under which the theme in reverse form is recognizable; later the eighth-note motif familiar from the transition group also enters. Characteristic for this passage is the accompanying, jagged horn-call. It is, however, only a preparation for the first climax of the development, in C minor, which now [m. 161] appears. Once more Mozart chooses counterpoint in its strictest guise: the theme is pursued three times in strettos through all four voices, the first two times with the same succession of voices, the third time with an interchanged succession; the theme given above, in a shortened version, serves as counterpoint. The harmonic framework, however, the constant succession of IV-V-$\frac{I}{IV}$-V-$\frac{I}{IV}$etc., receives a strong melodic heightening by the motif that appears in alternation in the winds:

23. For a "serial" analysis of this passage, see Hans Keller, *Strict Serial Technique in Classical Music*, in *Tempo*, 37 (Autumn 1955), 16 f. See also the excerpt from Jalowetz printed here (p. 99). [*Editor*]

Thus the unfolding drives finally into C-sharp minor, whose dominant, shimmering in the eighths of the violins, intensifies the agitation to the boiling point. Then, after the gruff deceptive cadence, the tired continuation in piano with the dejected theme in the winds [m. 188] is a genuinely Mozartean effect. But immediately thereafter the circle of fifths with renewed fury goes back to D major, the dominant of G minor. To be sure, the contrapuntal web slackens here, but to offset this the harmony changes each time on the fourth quarter note of the theme, whereby its effect is much enhanced, and at the same time two orchestral groups (violins and bassoon against basses and the other winds) knock against one another.

So the mighty torrent of passion falls back into its old riverbed in the recapitulation. There .is no clarification, no resignation, as there was in the first movement. It is therefore quite fitting that the main theme is brought back complete at the beginning of the recapitulation and the transition group cut to half its original extent, and that the whole movement is more and more exclusively given over to the key of G minor. The subordinate theme is the best illustration of this; in the new chromatic variations that its consequent now undergoes, it exploits the pain-filled atmosphere of this key to the point of self-torment, and the closing section, too, stamps its seal, dark and wild, on the whole.[24]

And so this symphony forms the sharpest expression of that deep, fatalistic pessimism which, latent in Mozart's nature from the beginning, struggled for artistic embodiment especially strongly in his last years. It is true that he was inwardly rich enough not to confine himself to this dark sphere from that time on. Nor did he ever return to it with the same relentless consistency. Rather, works like *Die Zauberflöte* and the Requiem, which mute that pessimism into a quieter but so much the deeper sorrow, teach us that even the experience of this symphony signifies only one station on the road of his spiritual development. Perhaps the change was only the result of the fact that Mozart here with relentless

24. The rhythm of the main theme
♩ | ♩ ♩ ♩ ♩ | ♩.
reappears once more in the winds here, as before; the two last strokes repeat its last two notes in augmentation.

energy drained that experience to its profoundest depths. The symphony has this reckless realism in common with *Don Giovanni*. Another
spiritual relationship [between the two works] is the lack of an ethical
quality in the sense of a Beethovenian, liberating solution. For Beethoven's kind of will, experiences of this sort bore within themselves the
struggle from its inception through its resolution, which took place in
the art-work itself. With Mozart this does not happen even in those
movements where he parts the clouds at the end. For him too liberation
ensued, but outside the work of art; in it he expressed the essence of the
creation demanding embodiment in a manner so heedless of consequences
that there was no further internal urge to create.

ALFRED HEUSS

~~~~~~~~~~~~~~~~~~

The Minor Second in Mozart's G minor Symphony †

Alfred Heuss (1877–1934) was a musicologist, critic, and editor. His article,
Das dämonische Element in Mozarts Werken, published in 1906 in the
Zeitschrift of the International Musical Society, was influential in under-
mining the strongly entrenched 19th-century conception of Mozart's music
as perfect in form but lacking in depth. The present essay is offered not
only for the light it throws on the G minor Symphony but also as an interesting example of a type of musical analysis called "hermeneutics." This
approach, favored principally by some German writers in the first decades
of this century, interprets the elements of a composition, such as intervals
and rhythms, in terms of emotions.

All higher existence is based on experience and perception. Neither one
without the other. One may experience without perceiving, and one
may attain perception without experiencing something. Neither one is
the truth, so that a synthesis is needed, resulting in a higher, third term,

† *Die kleine Sekunde in Mozarts g-moll Sinfonie,* in *Jahrbuch der Musikbibliothek
Peters für 1933,* Leipzig, 1934, pp. 54–66. With permission of the publishers, C. F.
Peters Corporation, 373 Park Avenue South, New York, N.Y. 10016. Translation by
the editor.

an experienced perception, or a perceived experience. In art this double unity, this synthesis, has a special importance. If art, no matter how varied its manifestation, were not experienced, it would be the most superfluous thing in the world and hardly conceivable even as sport. On the other hand, all deep insights in art are based on perceptions. The enjoyment of art, the mere experience of art, only coalesces when it is accompanied by a perception. This latter, however, must in turn be examined to determine whether it leads to a renewed, spiritualized experience, or any experience at all. If it does not, the perceptions have failed their most important test and in the end are not worth a straw. An example—and an important one: Hanslick's[1] definition of music as "form, sounding and in motion" is surely a perception, which will undoubtedly always have its adherents. But what happens when it is applied to human, artistic experience? Even the most convinced formalist will not want to assume that it is the "form, sounding and in motion" of a purely instrumental work that can arouse an audience to fever pitch. From this point of view Hanslick's conception of music, which lacks the opposite element of the synthesis and in addition had no living significance for its own author as a man of art, is impossible and, to quote Wagner's Biterolf, is "cheap, not worth a blow."

Nevertheless, we do not mean to say that experience always leads to enduring perceptions, even though, with one's own experience, it always comes to that in the end. The reverse can easily happen, that perceptions lead to experiences, and often of the deepest sort. When Parsifal, thoughtlessly slaying swans, has been enlightened about his deed and perceives what he has done, he attains his first experience, a strong one.[2] That's the way it goes countless times, and not only for callow youths. Any perception to which we are led from without, or from within ourselves, if it is genuine and finds us at all prepared, can lead to experiences of varying degrees of force. A genuine study of art, having as its purpose always to serve art, will consider one of its basic tasks to be to attain perceptions of this sort and to bring them to the experience of others. A good method for such a study to achieve this goal is through the examination of individual and very familiar works of art, which have been experienced countless times and by different generations, even though much that has been perceived about them is already available.

1. Concerning Hanslick, see below, p. 109. [*Editor*]
2. A reference to the scene in which Parsifal makes his first appearance in Wagner's opera. [*Editor*]

Let us now apply what has been said to Mozart's G minor Symphony. The "discovery" (perception) to be made here is very simple, so obvious that when it is stated everyone will immediately say that he has already noticed it and if not, it makes itself quite apparent. We do not have the slightest intention to deny this, but the fact is that there is no mention of it in the entire, not inconsiderable literature on the symphony, from Nägeli's [3] noteworthy remarks to our day, as for example in the lecture by Cherbuliez.[4] If the numerous authors had made the "discovery" but remained silent about it, their remarks indicate with absolute certainty that none of them had recognized or "perceived" it. For if they had perceived it, there would have followed practically automatically the further perception that the symphony operates in all four movements with the same device, a discovery that, if they had made it, would have placed all their comments on a quite different basis.

This small device, quite unpretentious but among the basic elements of music, is the *minor second,* the interval that, used appropriately, is the most painful one of our whole musical language. If I may speak personally, I should like to remark here, by way of introduction, and solely with respect to the whole matter of intervals: I made the observation at a time—about twenty years ago—when I had by no means begun working specifically with intervals, when I had only occasionally "experienced" their fundamental significance for the perception of many compositions, and had in no way recognized it yet. The "perception" grew out of frequent, strong "experience" of the symphony. Today, the situation with me is that if I approach the work as one unknown to me, I soon and unhesitatingly *must* arrive at the observation, and for no other reason than that I now have perceived the significance of intervals with respect to the part they can play in a work. I cannot here go into detail about so all-important a matter as the significance of intervals. Suffice it to say that this subject has not yet received adequate consideration, nor could it, because a fundamental fact has not been sufficiently realized: It is only possible to operate with these smallest components of the tonal language (and this is true for composers, too) if the interval in question finds some sort of fundamental application. To ascribe a special

---

3. Johann Georg Nägeli (1773–1836), was a Swiss composer, publisher, and writer. [Editor]

4. *Stilkritischer Vergleich von Mozarts beiden g-moll-Sinfonien von 1773 und 1788,* in *Bericht über die musikwissenschaftliche Tagung der . . . Mozarteum . . . 1931,* Leipzig, 1932, p. 112.***

significance to every fifth or fourth in a melody or theme would be entirely absurd, for many other reasons as well, a peculiarity that the musical language shares with the verbal language. In the latter, too, it matters
whether a word, no matter how important when taken by itself, is applied appropriately; if it is not, it may not even be heard.—Concerning
the tonal language of a genuinely organic work it may be remarked,
further, that a thematic interval important in our sense is expressed the
more clearly in the course of an extended movement, indeed of a whole
cyclic work, the more the composer gives it importance. As matters still
stand today, one must first ask whether the composer, and especially one
of the highest rank, did not work with the interval *unconsciously*. On this
subject we shall say here only that particularly for the composer of this
type the perception of his basic ideas is the most wonderful source of new
inspirations, whether these have to do with thematic working-out or
with the formation of new themes within this work. The remarks that
follow may be considered, from this point of view, a contribution to the
subject: What is conscious for the composer who is a genius?

The best expression for the first Allegro theme, it seems to me, is the
one coined by Ernst Lewicki,[5] an expression in which one immediately
recognizes the "experience"—namely, "ineffably grieving." That it is,
and the reason, expressed in musical terms, is in the special use of the
minor second. It is necessary to have studied much, from Monteverdi to
Wagner and Verdi, to be sufficiently aware of the painful character of
this interval. Each of the countless distinct cases is at the same time a
unique case, offering something special, and, for all its conformity, re-
quiring to be considered for its own sake. Here in the Mozart theme this
something special is of an extremely variegated sort. There is already
something decisive in the fact that the theme begins in the floating,
helpless region of the fifth, helpless also inasmuch as the long avoidance
of the tonic right at the beginning causes the theme to stand there without firm support. Notice, too, how seldom the tonic is touched in the
extended unfolding of the theme as it wanders on. The tonic does not
appear until the third measure of the theme, then not again until the
fourteenth.[6] Moreover the monotonous insistence on one tone, D, characterizes the opening of the theme throughout. Even without the second,

5. *Mozart's grosse sinfonische Trilogie*, in *Zeitschrift für Musik*, Oct. 1928.
6. Actually the twelfth. Heuss, however, seems to have overlooked the G in m. 10
of the theme. [*Editor*]

there is something definitely mournful in the sound, but only because it is the dominant. If presented as tonic, there is no mournfulness; on the contrary, the tonics have something resolute about them. For matters like this, real reasons cannot be given, because the subject really belongs to the metaphysics of music. Play the following:

What a quiet lamentation! What helplessness and loneliness! [7] How very different, however, this sounds:

It is almost necessary that one begin by realizing such things clearly, since my task consists precisely in making the reader, through certain aids comparable to a magnifying glass—which in this case would be a microscope—thoroughly aware of the grieving quality of the minor second employed here. And that this is in a certain sense very necessary is shown by the part that the symphony played with the Romantics, even a musician of the rank of a Robert Schumann, who was by no means alone in his opinion that the movement was governed by "lightness and grace." [8] Mozart's use of the second in the form of a "Mannheim sigh" is, at least in a certain sense, a phenomenon of the time; if it had been present in its pure form, the minor second and, with it, the grieving quality of the theme could not have been missed even by a Romantic. Let us listen therefore to this pure form, which—for study purposes— should be applied to all the versions of the principal theme:

7. For a long time I could not understand why the G minor melody of the Queen of the Night at the words "Zum Leiden bin ich auserkoren" made such a marked impression of helplessness on me. It results from the fact that the first tones lie in the fifth-register.

8. See Abert, *Mozart*, II, 579, footnote. [Here p. 70, footnote 1.—*Editor*]

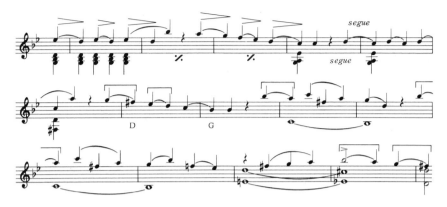

In this version[8a] the penultimate measure was anticipated, a measure before, by the viola, a fact that is not unimportant in performance:

The passage is also important because of the bass: For the first time the semitone is produced *chromatically,* and how essential a part is played in the course of the work by chromaticism, which is nothing else than the semitone principle consistently carried out, we shall have sufficient occasion to observe. Let us remember, however, that all its chromaticism goes back to the thematic semitone, such as that of the principal motif.

In the forte measures the minor second, though at first half-concealed in the oboes:

has already become a permanent harmonic ingredient, as a tension-creating interval in cadences. Another reason—a solidly founded one—for relating this to our second is that later, in the last movement, the same cadence-seconds are built into the theme itself. Thus in the first movement everything lies prepared, so to speak, that will become essen-

8a. In mm. 9 and 11 of his example, Heuss has d^2 and $f\sharp^2$ for the last two quarters. [*Editor*]

tial to the treatment of the later movements. Here in the first movement the determined forte measures signify the first firm invitation to oppose pain, with resolute, consequently cadencing, seconds. That this invitation has, and can have, no results is shown by the immediate return of the main theme.

For the most part this is diatonic, but contains within it chordal components that in the B-flat major subsidiary theme [m. 28] are drawn in to offer powerful resistance. This resistance might have constituted a halfway decisive counterbalance, if the thorn of the seconds had not penetrated too deep. As early as in the seventh measure of this theme it again exerts its sting. Consider:

Is not the thorn also embedded in this theme, which began so powerfully, so completely free of dissonance? The chordal theme, however, is important precisely in this respect and with its ascending chord-tones in the third measure has uncommon significance for the formation of the main theme of the finale. We find it already in the basses, with its upbeat of a fourth, in the development (m. 194): [9]

And let us anticipate by noticing how in the final theme this leap serves as a springboard but suddenly the second, the *ton fixe* of the symphony, is again present.

Are we really surprised to find our second as a melodic chromatic component of the second theme, right in the first notes, after which it disappears for three measures, only to wield its poisonous needle later more vigorously? I cite only:

9. Actually, the passage illustrated does not appear until the recapitulation, m. 204. [*Editor*]

Incidentally, the second, purely chromatic motif returns, but "de-poisoned," in the Minuet of the *Jupiter Symphony*.

Not only the subsidiary theme, at its beginning courageous unto death, then, but also the second theme is "poisoned" by the minor second, so that composition textbooks can now count the movement among the rare examples in which all the themes are thematically related to one another. The second theme must now, in order to make manifest its true character, of course be regarded in the recapitulation as a theme in minor and also because some marked alterations are made in it. I must now leave a great deal to the investigation of the now initiated observer, with the advice not to take the task lightly. The connecting measure (m. 51), for example, is according to its true nature to be understood thus:

It could quite well, since it has approximately that effect, have been:

the exact form in which it appears in the above-mentioned Minuet of the C major Symphony (second part). I mention this example even though it is unimportant in itself, to make clear how consciously even a subordinate connecting motif is immersed in seconds, whether one senses them or not.

In the context there is something moving about the suddenly appearing A-flat major dominant-seventh seconds. Their character as dominant removes all grief and sharpness, the latter because the chord rests on the root, not on the third as a sixth chord, a point to which we shall return. For four measures there is delicious repose; the second is there, but it is as though this inflicter of pain had been deprived by a magic spell of all power to hurt. Artful repose! For there is a great rousing up in the immediately following measures, whose continuation again introduces something new, chromaticism in a most energetic-painful ascent (see *a*):

The means of withstanding pain, with ascending chromaticism in a technically skilled construction—syncopation along with staccato quarter notes—are knowingly employed here. Right alongside (at *b*) we experience an inspired, sudden bringing together of the painful main thematic intervals, the minor second and minor sixth, in a strongly energetic outbreak. And actually the successful result seems to follow at once, the beautifully ordered scale figure on major chords descending like a happy augury. One expects a confirmation, if only for the sake of "form." What does appear, however—though in B-flat major; or rather *precisely* in B-flat major?

The second is there again, brought into the "form" literally, namely "wound up" three times, linked together with itself, thus manifesting itself as the most central component of the movement.

It is not my intention to follow the development in its unfolding; nor is it necessary for our purpose, since there is not a measure in which the second-motif does not appear. We shall consider briefly only the twelve measures leading to the recapitulation, because here every last possibility is squeezed out of the minor second in its function as suspension, at first as fundamental motif in the original fifth-register by the basses, then in the violins, then in the woodwinds—here however in a crawling, compressed chromaticism, with the motif split into two semitones. The measures:

with their doubled chromaticism [10] move as though they were "quarter-tone music," the sound of grief would melt a heart of stone—a transition to the principal section, in which a more intensive employment of the minor second would be inconceivable.

Despite the considerable space occupied by chromaticism in this symphony, it could be called a chromatic work only indirectly, for it has become more and more clear to us that all the chromaticism derives from the minor second—the latter is consequently primary, the former a result. So deeply does the minor second as a sound of grief penetrate in Mozart that even successions of semitones must make their appearance out of deepest need. This is especially important for the second movement.

Characteristic for that movement, at first, is the interval of decision, the fourth leading to the tonic, a feature of the two later movements also, and an uncommonly important one in so far as it indicates with the greatest certainty (which is confirmed by the content of the movements) that they all wish to turn away from the second—hence the leap of a fourth—though the second somehow continues to appear with a fatalistic persistence. Now, supported by the firmness of the fourth, a struggle against pain begins. We did not find a true conflict in the first movement, nor could we, since all the themes were "infected" by the minor second; the movement, taken as a whole, is one of pain, it is grief itself. It showed, however, various ways in which pain might perhaps be avoided. And it is with these that the other three movements concern themselves.

It is of course no accident that the second movement is in the key of the cheery previous symphony, in E-flat major, for it might quite readily have been a movement in B-flat major. Mozart wants to go to his happiness-inducing E-flat major region, to rest, to forget himself. And to feel secure in doing so, he seizes upon a special means, one of his most firmly established favorite ideas, which later forms the main theme of the finale of the *Jupiter Symphony*. It is quite as though one wanted to put on special armor in order to be protected against something. Let us listen to the theme in its purity:

10. The C♯ in the second measure of Heuss's example, which is not in Mozart's autograph, seems to have been added in some 19th-century editions. [*Editor*]

The assured theme, at home in earlier, more robust eras, is revealed here in all clarity, and yet, what peers out at us with quiet dread through its unfolding in six monotonous eighth notes? The beginning of the symphony, as it was given in our first example, without the suspensions of seconds. And does not the second as crawling chromatic begin to stir as early as the second measure, down in the basses, and further, has not the second already forced its way into the theme itself in the fourth measure?

What can we expect later, if the second already lurks in the opening measures? But Mozart still "notices" nothing; the phrase of happy love from *Idomeneo,* still happier later in *Die Zauberflöte,* appears (mm. 5 and 6), but then, after a frightened and completely unexpected stroke of lightning in thirty-second notes, the minor second is again before us:

Here is our second, in all its purity and sharply accented, also led chromatically downward, in a state of suffering. How quickly we have reached the disintegration of the theme that began with such security, and, what is especially remarkable, how precisely we can follow the process of disintegration! Concerning the pure second-motif, which now appears not as suspension but as cadencing dominant interval, the reader is reminded of what has been said above; the genuinely Mozartean sixth chord provides the needed sharpness. For the rest we shall be as brief as possible. The C♭-second so deliberately introduced in m. 11 will now not be ignored. From here on we notice a lightening of the mood again to about m. 24, where a sudden transformation occurs in the thirty-second-note motif: up to that point a motif of a third, it must now permit itself to be recast to the second-motif of the opening movement and as such to gain the upper hand, though not exclusive dominance.

I have discussed in some detail in another place [11] the beginning of

11. *Über den Vortrag einiger Motive und Stellen in klassischen Werken, vornehmlich Mozarts,* in *Zeitschrift für Musik,* Aug. 1931.

the second section with its appearance of the "stone guest" and the chromatic ascent of the six-tone principal motif, which must now however be considered in connection with the opening theme of the symphony also. The effect of these measures must be carefully observed; it manifests itself especially in the crawling chromaticism of the first bass motif, which now pursues its destiny quite openly in the high register, in measure 73 filling three octaves. Something quite new is presented in the recapitulation, where this motif is extended by an additional second and now speaks to us as a most gripping recitative-monologue; these are measures Mozart never duplicated in his instrumental music. In measures 84 and 85 the second violin "speaks":

in measure 88 the first violin "answers":

And here, with this unspeakably sad, hopeless "answer" we experience something entirely new again, the collision of seconds in "space," which, as we shall see, becomes a cardinal point of the Minuet and which will be discussed in connection with that movement. Up to now we have experienced the second temporally, in melodic progression, but now as a dissonance of seconds—though at first at the distance of a ninth. Actual seconds we encounter too, in measure 104, when the tones E♭ and F♭—an anticipation of the famous *Eroica* dissonance—sound together. We are now prepared, at least to a certain extent, for the Minuet.

The essence of that movement resides in this: With enormous, most embittered energy Mozart seeks to overcome pain, the interval of a second. In the first section he seems to have accomplished this, for the interval of a second is apparently brushed aside by the now most powerful opening leap of a fourth. But only apparently! In the forephrase of the theme, as we outline it, the second is there as clear as day:

And how it springs forward at the end, chromatically, and, it seems to me, downright scornfully!

But now the second section, one of the most extraordinary contrapuntal passages in the whole literature. Here begins a struggle, a conflict with the second as hard and relentless as any ever waged. The collision of the tones D and E♭ is deliberately engineered throughout, the leap of a seventh to E♭ indicating a wild audaciousness. To satisfy purely compositional requirements the violins could have played merely:

But Mozart wanted the hard, pitiless simultaneity, prepared in the second movement; it is as though he wanted to drown out one pain with a stronger one. As is well known, the setting, at first purely two-part—a contrapuntal event that ranks with anything Bach wrote—sounds like a full-textured one, the reason being, besides the satanic energy, the layout in triple octaves. The Trio, free from pain and inclined to joy, must also be understood from the standpoint of drowning out sorrow. The allusion to seconds is hardly felt as such.

While the fourth of decision reaches only to the tonic in the second movement and to the third in the Minuet, but then over fifth and octave to the tenth, the theme of the finale completes this development by reaching the tenth in a single, and rather light, leap. Indeed one has the impression that the energy of the leap extends even farther. But, as though with the freezing glance of a basilisk, the second, most strikingly introduced, brings the charge to a halt. This interval is now clearly visible as the headpiece of the theme itself, no longer a suspension but a dissonance integrated into the chord, and deliberately presented as a seventh or ninth. Mozart had exploited the harsh cry of the minor ninth in the G minor Quintet too; in the course of the present movement it plays its part out with a positively desperate fanaticism. A special effect is created in the onrushing theme-opening by the soft dynamic. Actually, one expects forte, as in the Minuet, with piano contrast for the next two measures. But matters are reversed, and a contrast-dynamic employed of a tightness never previously heard:

At *b*) the effect is not of the second as such but merely cadential. But the passionate use of the cadence with its narrow intervals is even less accidental than in the first forte measures of the first movement. On one side the wide chordal ascent with the very sudden appearance of the fatalistic second, on the other an equally fatalistic decisive forte discharge of almost nothing but semitones, even though they reveal no pain in their cadencing. But that is precisely the point. The minor second is there, as a cruel fact; it does not allow itself to be avoided any more than an incurable illness would. It returns in every movement, in ever-new shapes. In the Minuet it was annealed to the form; now Mozart, while by no means proof against its sudden bursting forth—its appearance as headpiece of the chordal motif shows this—stands *above* pain. As in the Minuet he has done what Leibniz did, who smothered a frightful physical pain by a still more tormenting one. And so Mozart wrestles formally with the second, presenting it simultaneously in three voices at the dissonance of a ninth:

There is objectivization in this procedure, and if the whole third section now races on in a constant forte until the entrance of the second theme, it does so in closed scale-passages and chordal figures whose form has been forged by the second—notice the winds—with the thematic cadence-motif (*b*) built in. This does not create a situation like the one in the Trio of the Minuet, but it does result in the painful and forceful situation we experience in the closed third section.

The true aspect of things is shown us this time by the second theme, in B-flat major, which, however, even more than the one in the first movement, must be considered in its minor version. Not only because it is only there that it reveals its real nature as well as its destination, but because Mozart made the most marked alterations in it, with a view to bringing out the seconds even more strongly. Positively touching is the weary, almost worn out chromatic song of the bassoons (mm. 262–267).[12] And previously, in the violins, I see in:

a man writhing in pain. Now that the principle has been pointed out, I must ask the reader to proceed by himself with respect to details and particularly with respect to the development section. There, once more great sorrow breaks out with daemonic force; significantly, the sharply drawn cadence motif is lacking, while the chordal motif, now presented forte and storming up to the second, celebrates orgies and pursues the tormented man into the most remote keys. That frightful music like this has been peacefully "enjoyed" as "development music" for a hundred years indicates plainly the blunting of sensitivity to feeling that befell the 19th century, so that stronger and stronger external stimuli are required for feeling to be aroused. This symphony of Mozart's is thoroughly aristocratic in the 18th-century sense. It really addresses only aristocratic individuals of a spiritual cast who have already experienced in some way, and at the same time learned to deal with, what this work expresses. Alongside this work only the other two symphonies by Mozart should be heard, in exactly the order in which they were written—our symphony consequently in the center. Observe, with our conclusions in mind, its close. The resigned cadence motif is fully instated, together with—something quite new in this movement—the similarly firmly established organic scale. But how jangling the dissonances that appear with it:

What a development from the helplessly grieving suspension-second of the chaotic first movement, bearing within itself everything that was

12. Heuss has mm. 253–258, but this is an obvious miscalculation. [*Editor*]

to happen later, to this metallically jangling close! This symphony, and only this one, is Mozart's *Eroica;* only as such and only within the trilogy is it to be fully understood and properly valued.

It was not my intention to offer a psychic analysis of the work; if nevertheless something has been said about that aspect too, it has only been as a necessary but subsidiary matter. My aim has been nothing more than to call attention to that most distinctive interval which, in the truest sense of the word, gives this unique symphonic work its "tone." At the same time, I have shown that this interval permeates the symphony in all four of its movements, thematically, but also that the second undergoes all sorts of development. That further psychic-musical investigations of the work may be undertaken from this point of view, from the clear perception of this germ-cell, will be substantiated by anyone who knows what a very important germ-cell means in a living organism. Our investigation, however, has a second goal. It aims to draw attention with full emphasis to a completely neglected field in musical composition as well as in the perception of musical art-works—that of the significance of intervals. Some indications of the correct "use" of this study have been given previously. There are innumerable and important works in which no interval plays a particularly significant part, but countless others in which one does. And if we here now only mention, in passing, that the most joyful interval, the major sixth, and, connected with it, broad chordal themes, etc., give a special stamp to the first symphony of Mozart's symphonic trilogy, the one in E-flat major, this simple observation points a new way to further study of that work, which moreover will lead to passages that reveal direct connections with our symphony and also with the *Jupiter.* Finally it is always quite simple observations and perceptions, presenting themselves openly, in art and science as well as in life, that reveal to us new aspects in what has long been familiar and often experienced.

HEINRICH JALOWETZ

[*Twelve-Tone Writing in Mozart*] †

We must resort to an even more boldly inventive inner ear than Wagner's to find a genuine twelve-tone line in the past: the unison passage at the beginning of the development of the Finale of Mozart's Symphony in G Minor.

If we follow this line from C on the third beat of measure 2 to measure 9 and disregard the slide before measure 5, we get a series of ten tones of the chromatic scale that are treated as of equal value and therefore not as in traditional chromaticism. We can, of course, supply a harmonic progression consisting of purely diatonic modulation rather than of a mere sequence of diminished-seventh chords; but the fact that Mozart presents the line in unison shows that he conceived it more from the purely melodic standpoint * * * What makes the example from Mozart so unusual is the ruthless, overlapping sequence, which appears four times and contains a three-note group (made of a diminished fourth and diminished seventh) that has no diatonic point of support. For a fleeting moment the sequence escapes from the gravity of diatonic (tonal) space and sets up a genuine chromatic (atonal) segment. In addition, the pas-

† From *On the Spontaneity of Schoenberg's Music*, in *The Musical Quarterly,* XXX (1944), 387; by permission of G. Schirmer, Inc.

sage is a constructive part of the whole, for it is a transition leading into a key remote from the point of departure. * * * In Mozart's remarkable passage, the harmonic dissolution is further intensified by the rhythmic dissolution. This carefree leap into unexplored musical territory is justified by its very boldness.

ARNOLD SCHOENBERG

[*The Transition in the First Movement*] †

Schoenberg singles out the extension of the transition section in the first movement of our symphony as "one of the most interesting" examples of producing contrast between tonic and tonic in a recapitulation. He sums up the events in question in the outline given here. The symbols in the example have these meanings: t = tonic minor; M = mediant major; SM = submediant major; subt = subtonic minor.

† From *Structural Functions of Harmony*, New York, 1954, p. 144. Copyright 1954 by W. W. Norton & Company, Inc.

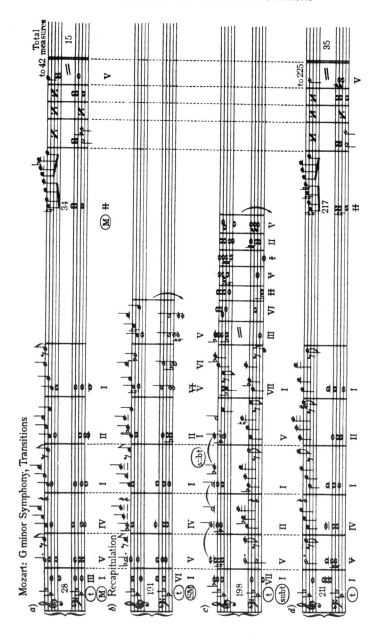

VIEWS AND COMMENTS

The comments on the work have been selected with a view to showing the changing attitudes towards Mozart in the course of the 19th and 20th centuries.

F. J. FÉTIS[†]

~~~~~

Although the luxury of a large orchestra was not available to Mozart for his Symphony in G minor, and although the massive effects that astonish and transport us in Beethoven's symphonies are not found here, the invention that sparkles in this work, the impassioned and energetic expression that suffuses it, and the melancholy color that dominates it make of it one of the most beautiful creations of the human spirit. If this symphony had been orchestrated in the modern fashion, and if to the power of delightful song, of exquisite sensibility, and of elegant and pure harmony found here had been added that of a very intense sonority, the work would have been beyond all comparison.

ALEXANDRE OULIBICHEFF

~~~~~

[*The G minor Symphony*] [††]

Now come the last and most perfect creations of Mozart in the symphonic category: the works in G minor and in C. These are almost twin sisters, since they were born only a month apart. Both incomparably beautiful, these sisters nevertheless differ in their features as much as

[†] From a review of a concert in Paris, May 11, 1828, in *Revue musicale,* III (1828), 372. Translation by the editor. Fétis (1784–1871), a Belgian musicologist, composer, and critic, was founder and editor of the *Revue.*

[††] Alexandre Oulibicheff (1794–1858), *Nouvelle biographie de Mozart,* Moscow, 1843, pp. 255–60. Translation by the editor. The author, a Russian official, was an enthusiastic musical amateur. In his three-volume work on Mozart he held up that composer as the apogee of musical art, Beethoven representing a decline into anarchy.

in their character. A dilettante of the 18th century compared the younger to Minerva, escorted by Apollo and the muses, and the elder to Venus, weeping for the death of Adonis; he had recognized in the latter all the qualities of the heart, in the former all the gifts of the spirit.

The Symphony in G minor, like the Quintet in the same key, expresses the agitation of passion, the desires and regrets of an unhappy love, but it expresses them with the difference that in the quintet there is a plaint locked in the depths of the soul, or at most poured into the bosom of a friend, while in the symphony there is a grief unrestrained and limitless, which it proclaims to the entire world, wishing to fill the world with its lamentations. It is the difference between an elegy and an elegiac ode. Another distinction to be observed between the two works is that the psychological drama of the quintet * * * has a happy ending; the finale of the symphony, on the other hand, marks the culminating point of suffering, a despair mingled with rage. There is a progression here that is interrupted only by the Andante, the character of which must always differ noticeably from that of the other movements if the listener is not to be bored and the effect lost by a continuous insistence upon the same expression. Listen to the opening of the first Allegro, that motif marked with a melancholy charm that has engraved it in the memory of all music-lovers. It is at first only a veiled sadness, a sweet and tender melancholy, but it becomes bitter and poignant in the second reprise.[1] Immediately after the tonic chord that begins this reprise, and by a transition in which an F♮, changed mentally into an E♯, achieves the magical effect, the theme returns in F-sharp minor.[2] It reappears, but full of hesitation and uneasiness, seeking asylum in the most diverse keys but finding it nowhere; then wrestling in desperation with a formidable countersubject in the violins and bass; then, consumed by so much painful effort, it appears abbreviated, suffocated, to fall in tatters, to expire slowly on a succession of split imitations and swooning harmonies; then finally here it is reborn in its original form and the symphony begins again. Beautiful, sublime,—and cursed be the poverty of the language that does not offer me any other laudatory and admiring epithets for this more than admirable composition of the middle section of the movement.

1. That is, the development section. [*Editor*]
2. When this symphony was played for the first time at the Paris Conservatoire, the whole assemblage of musical savants, says M. Fétis, uttered a cry of enthusiasm at this sublime modulation.

But what dream escaped through the ivory gates of Elysium, or rather what hope, indefinite and distant, comes to arrest the course of this suffering and to comfort the soul, like a divine balm applied to its wounds? Andante 6/8, E-flat major, one of those ineffable works where all is revelation for the feelings and mystery for the spirit. The theme is a little vague in contour, complex in form, and it is precisely from these qualities that the movement derives the magic of its effect and an angelic expression that touches on the supernatural. One must examine it closely to be convinced that this masterpiece, as varied and as rich in patterns as it may appear, was entirely constructed out of the opening four measures, plus another idea inseparable from the theme though of an entirely different aspect. This is a little figure in thirty-second notes, grouped in pairs, which is heard ceaselessly flickering and mingling its butterfly flutter with the gravest syncopations, the most chromatic harmonic progressions, the most unexpected modulatory excursions, the most abstruse workings-out of the theme. Add a limpid and prismatic instrumentation, where the same details are colored by a multitude of different tints according to whether they are allotted to string or wind parts; and, at the center of this harmonious fermentation, some phrases of song that come to you from heaven, like whiffs of a breeze charged with scent. The composer has signed the piece in great capital letters: Wolfgang Amadeus Mozart, just as he signed the Andante of the E-flat major Quartet, the Andantes of the Quartets in C major and A major, the Adagio of the Quintet in D. Shall we ever see a counterfeiter skillful enough to imitate this signature, inimitable up to now?

The Minuet, Allegro 3/4, recalls us to the positive character and the general tonality of the symphony. What a masterpiece, in a few lines, is this minuet! What wild melancholy, tempered by a certain haughty abandon, breathes from this song in minor, what enticing warmth and pathetic verve in the canon that occupies the other half of the piece, and what the musician has built with the theme broken into two figures and led, in a double movement, across the surrounding neighboring tones; how deliciously, finally, after the vehemence and tumult of this sublime travail, the plaintive, weeping coda of wind instruments ends the piece by repeating the theme softly and on a chromatic bass! We do not know anything more beautiful or more moving among works of this kind.

In the Mozartean symphonies the effect of what is called the trio is calculated in a manner relative to and subordinate to that of the Menuetto, with the aim of creating a diversion or establishing a contrast, with respect♭to expression as much as to style. These trios are always some measures of solo writing, given to the wind instruments, some graceful and light cantilenas in a melodic style. It should not be forgotten that they occupy the center of the movement and it is always the repetition of the minuet that is given for the conclusion.

The moving, yet half resigned, plaint that characterizes the Minuet is followed by the accents of despair in the finale, Allegro assai 2/4. Tired of suffering, the soul grows angry and revolts against torment; it abandons itself to an impetuous rage, which approaches ferocity by the accentuation of octaves and of trills in the phrase that follows the motif. With a thematic foundation of this nature, the subordinate ideas must naturally be softer, because it was impossible to intensify the basic material, and moreover because the law of contrast demands it. However, no matter how difficult the obstacles that these ideas encounter on their way, no matter what harmonic complications they are obliged to traverse in their repetitions, they are always recognizable as necessary episodes or as variants of one and the same song of imprecations and despair. I doubt that there is in music anything more profoundly incisive, more cruelly painful, more violently desperate, more atrociously impassioned, than the second reprise of this finale. And to achieve so exuberant an expression Mozart used scarcely any other means than the theme, whose outline disposed at the beginning over the intervals of the harmonic triad, is here deployed on the intervals of the chord of the minor ninth and other acrid harmonies. Here too the theme is divided, in canon, between the two sections of the orchestra, in its furious march clashing against hostile countersubjects and soon overwhelmed by them; then, conquering in its turn, it is heard beating pitilessly and without rest on a progression of chromatic chords that mount by one sharp after another to the opposite extreme of its original key, and this continues for eighty measures. From what event of his inner life, from what paroxysm of the heart, did Mozart draw this delirious and at the same time so classic inspiration, and how did this overflow of passion burst out of this overflow of science? The second part [3] of the finale even surpasses the first, in that the episodic songs that appeared first in B-flat, the relative major, now return in the tonic, where their more moving or more agitated expression enters more decidedly into the general color of the movement and pleases the ear much better. There is hardly a finale to which *finis coronat opus* would be more applicable, or a work to which it would be more difficult

3. I.e. the recapitulation. [*Editor*]

to apply it than the Symphony in G minor, a composition so elevated and so energetic from its beginning.

EDUARD HANSLICK†

Independently of the fact that our feelings can never become the basis of aesthetic laws, there are many cogent reasons why we should not trust to the feelings aroused by music. As a consequence of our mental constitution, words, titles, and other conventional associations (in sacred, military, and operatic music more especially) give to our feelings and thoughts a direction which we often falsely ascribe to the character of the music itself. For, in reality, there is no causal nexus between a musical composition and the feelings it may excite, as the latter vary with our experience and impressibility. The present generation often wonder how their forefathers could imagine that just this arrangement of sounds adequately represented just this feeling. We need but instance the effects which works by Mozart, Beethoven, and Weber produced when they were new as compared with their effects on us. How many compositions by Mozart were thought by his contemporaries to be the most perfect expressions of passion, warmth, and vigor of which music is capable! The placidity and moral sunshine of Haydn's symphonies were placed in contrast with the violent bursts of passion, the internal strife, the bitter and acute grief embodied in Mozart's music.[1] Twenty or thirty years later, precisely the same comparison was made between Beethoven and Mozart. Mozart, the emblem of supreme and transcendent passion, was replaced

---

† From *The Beautiful in Music*, Leipzig, 1854, transl. by Gustav Cohen, New York, 1891. Hanslick (1825–1904), influential critic and professor of music at the University of Vienna, became famous for the book from which our abstract is taken. The thesis of his book is that music is incapable of expressing any specific feelings or emotions and that the beauty of music arises from its own "form" and "ideas."

1. Of Rochlitz in particular there are sayings on record about Mozart's instrumental music which sound rather strange to our ears. This same Rochlitz describes the graceful *minuet-capriccio* in Weber's "Sonata in A flat" as "the copious, incessant effusion of a passionate and fiercely agitated mind, controlled, withal, by a marvelous steadiness of purpose."

by Beethoven, while he himself was promoted to the Olympic classicality
of Haydn. Every observant musician will, in the course of his own life,
experience analogous changes of taste. The musical merit of the many
compositions which at one time made so deep an impression, and the
aesthetic enjoyment which their originality and beauty still yield, are not
altered in the least by this dissimilar effect on the feelings at different
periods. Thus, there is no invariable and inevitable nexus between musical works and certain states of mind; the connection being, on the contrary, of a far more transient kind than in any other art.

SIR GEORGE GROVE†

I cannot find in this beautiful movement [the first movement of the
G minor Symphony] the distress which some critics have discovered—'a
tide of suffering which can flow in few hearts without bursting them.'
Pathetic it is, no doubt, but there is something in the definite regularity
with which its various sections and even the sentences of its themes are
laid out, that gives a more formal character to the music than we now
associate with grief.

DONALD FRANCIS TOVEY††

The sonata style never lost for him [Mozart] its dramatic character, but,
while it was capable of pathos, excitement, and even vehemence, it

† From *Mozart's Symphony in G minor,* in *The Musical Times,* XLVIII (1907),
25. Grove (1820–1900) was the first director of the Royal College of Music in London
and editor of the great *Dictionary of Music and Musicians.*

†† From *Sonata Forms,* in *Encyclopedia Britannica,* 11th ed., New York, 1911,
Vol. XXV, p. 396. Composer, conductor, and pianist, Tovey (1875–1940) is best known
today for his brilliant *Essays in Musical Analysis* (6 vols.) and other writings.

could not concern itself with catastrophes or tragic climaxes. The G minor symphony shows poignant feeling, but its pathos is not that of a tragedy; it is there from first to last as a result, not a foreboding nor an embodiment, of sad experiences. In the still more profound and pathetic G minor quintet we see Mozart for once transcending his limits.

GUIDO ADLER

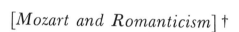

[*Mozart and Romanticism*] †

In each of the Classic masters there is a bit of the Romantic, and that is why writers who have studied the matter from this point of view have lumped them with the Romantics. E. T. A. Hoffmann does this on the basis of his argument that "instrumental music is the most Romantic of all arts." He himself was a disciple of Mozart in music, and bobbed gently in the Romantic tide. A whole series of composers oscillated between Classicism and Romanticism. Of the Classic composers Mozart exerted the strongest and most lasting influence on musical Romanticism. Individual works contain fundamental traits of Romanticism—the G minor Symphony, for example. It must not be overlooked, however, that it stands between the E-flat major and C major Symphonies. Mozart's leaning towards color, his modulation—which uses more and more mediants the further it progresses, a procedure that Beethoven surely adopted from him— Mozart's favoring of irregular rhythms, these among other things explain his support by the adherents and representatives of the Romantic movement. The theme of the G minor Symphony and the second theme of the Clarinet Quintet are the harbingers of Romanticism.

† From Guido Adler, ed., *Handbuch der Musikgeschichte*, 2nd ed., 1929 (reprinted 1961 by Musikverlag Hans Schneider), II, 793 f. Translation by the editor. Adler (1880–1941), one of the pioneer Austrian musicologists, succeeded Hanslick at the University of Vienna. He is best known now as editor (and one of the authors) of the *Handbuch* and as editor of the great collection *Denkmäler der Tonkunst in Österreich* (Monuments of Music in Austria).

ALFRED EINSTEIN[†]

This is the symphony without drums and trumpets; what would those festive instruments be doing in this fatalistic piece of chamber music? Nowhere does Mozart's independence of Haydn show itself so strikingly as in this work. His inexorableness contrasts sharply with the cheerful optimism of Haydn, who never stuck to the key of D minor or C minor, say, through even one whole first movement, let alone three whole movements, including the Finale. Even the turn to B-flat major in the exposition of the first movement has something both fierce and weary about it, and when, in the recapitulation, the flute, bassoon, and strings return to the minor, they do so with the finality of the pronouncement of Minos. The same is true of the last movement; the finality of both is the result of their developments, which are unlike any Haydn ever wrote. For these developments are plunges into the abyss of the soul, symbolized in modulations so bold that to Mozart's contemporaries they must have seemed to lose their way entirely, and so distant that only Mozart himself could find the path back from them into the light of day. It is strange how easily the world has accepted such a work and has even been able to think of it as a document of 'Grecian lightness and grace'—a characterization that could apply at best only to the divine tranquillity of the Andante or to the trio of the Minuet, otherwise so heroically tragic.

† From Alfred Einstein, *Mozart, His Character, His Work,* transl. by Arthur Mendel and Nathan Broder, New York: Oxford University Press, 1945, p. 235. Einstein (1880–1952), one of the greatest Mozart authorities of his or any other time, drastically revised Köchel's catalogue of Mozart's works for its third edition (1937), on which the current sixth edition is based.

Bibliography

From the vast literature on Mozart, the following are selected as basic.

MOZART'S LIFE, WORK, LETTERS

Abert, Hermann, *W. A. Mozart,* 7th ed., 2 vols., Leipzig, 1956.
   Still one of the best biographies and one of the two most comprehensive and authoritative studies of the works. It is a drastic revision of Otto Jahn's biography and was first published in 1919–21, as the 5th ed. of that work. The 7th ed. is essentially a reprint of the 5th; a third volume, incorporating corrections and additions, was announced as in preparation in 1955. There is unfortunately no English translation.
Anderson, Emily, *The Letters of Mozart and His Family,* 3 vols., London, 1938; 2nd ed., 2 vols., New York, 1966.
   A selection from this work was published by Eric Blom as *Mozart's Letters* in a Penguin edition, 1956. Generous quotations from the letters are a feature of W. J. Turner's *Mozart, The Man and His Works,* revised ed., New York, 1966.
Deutsch, Otto Erich, *Mozart, a Documentary Biography,* transl. by Eric Blom, Peter Branscombe, and Jeremy Noble, Stanford, Calif., 1965.
Einstein, Alfred, *Mozart, His Character, His Work,* transl. by Arthur Mendel and Nathan Broder, New York, 1945.
Köchel, Ludwig Ritter von, *Chronologisch-thematisches Verzeichnis sämtlicher Tonwerke Wolfgang Amadé Mozarts,* 6th ed., Wiesbaden, 1964.
   The celebrated thematic catalogue of Mozart's works, first published in 1862 at Leipzig.
Schneider, Otto, and Anton Algatzy, *Mozart-Handbuch,* Vienna, 1962.
   Especially useful as a guide through the literature.
Wyzewa, Théodore de, and G. de Saint-Foix, *Wolfgang Amédée Mozart,* 5 vols., Paris, 1912–46.
   This is the other comprehensive study of the works. Each one is examined in detail. The last 3 vols. are by Saint-Foix alone.

THE SYMPHONIES

In addition to the relevant sections of the books listed above, the following studies are recommended:

Larsen, Jens Peter, *The Symphonies,* in H. C. Robbins Landon and Donald Mitchell, eds., *The Mozart Companion,* New York, 1956, pp. 156–99.

Saint-Foix, G. de, *The Symphonies of Mozart,* transl. by Leslie Orrey, London, 1947.